Content

50 AWESOME DIP RECIPES 4

1. Almond Dip Recipe 4
2. BUFFALO CHICKEN WING DIP Recipe 4
3. Baked Spinach Crab And Artichoke Dip Recipe 4
4. Baked Spinach Artichoke Dip Recipe 5
5. Bongo Dip Recipe 5
6. Braunschweiger Dips Recipe 5
7. CROCK POT BEAN DIP Recipe 6
8. Cajun Cheese Dip Recipe 6
9. California Bean Dip Recipe 6
10. Catalina Dip Recipe 6
11. Cheese Dip Recipe 7
12. Cheesy Spinach Bacon Dip Recipe 7
13. Chili Cheese Dip Recipe 7
14. Chilled Crab Dip Recipe 7
15. Corn Bread Dip Recipe 8
16. Cottage Cheese Dip Recipe 8
17. Fiesta Corn Dip Recipe 8
18. Football Dip Recipe 8
19. Franks RedHot Buffalo Chicken Dip Recipe 9
20. Hissy Fit Dip Recipe 9
21. Hot As Devil Pitchfork Pepper Dip Recipe 9
22. Hot Sausage Party Dip Recipe 10
23. Hot Spinach Dip Recipe 10
24. Janets Black Bean Salsa Recipe 10
25. Jimmy Dean Dip Recipe 11
26. Knorr Spinach Dip Recipe 11
27. Mexican Sausage Dip Recipe 11
28. Ms. Pringles Bean Dip Recipe 11
29. New Mexico Spinach Dip Recipe 12
30. Queso Dip Recipe 12
31. Ranch Bean Dip Recipe 12
32. Ro Tel Dip Recipe 13
33. Rootie Tootie Party Bean Dip Recipe 13
34. Ruben Dip Recipe 13
35. Sausage Beef Rotel Dip Recipe 13
36. Sausage Dip Recipe 14
37. Spicey Sausage Cream Cheese Dip Recipe 14
38. Spicy Cheese Dip Recipe 14
39. Spicy Sau...
40. Super Bo...
41. Super Bo...
42. Super Sausage Dip Recipe 16
43. Sweet Tomato Chutney Recipe 16
44. Ultimate Spinach Dip Recipe 16
45. Vegetable Dip Recipe 17
46. Velveeta Rotel Dip Recipe 17
47. Weasel Dip Recipe 17
48. Zesty Salsa Recipe 17
49. Buffalo Chicken Dip Recipe 18
50. Creamy Italian Dip Recipe 18

INDEX 20
CONCLUSION 22

50 Awesome Dip Recipes

***

1. Almond Dip Recipe

Serving: 8 | Cook: 10mins

Ingredients

- 1-1/2 cups grated swiss cheese
- 1 packet cream cheese softened
- 1/3 cup salad dressing
- 1/3 cup toasted sliced almonds
- 2 tablespoons chopped green onion

Direction

- Combine cheeses, dressing and green onion then place in deep casserole.
- Spread almonds over top and bake 15 minutes at 350.
- After 8 minutes remove from oven and stir.

2. BUFFALO CHICKEN WING DIP Recipe

Serving: 8 | Cook: 30mins

Ingredients

- 2 (8 ounce) packages cream cheese, softened
- 3/4 cup hot pepper sauce
- 1 cup Ranch-style salad dressing
- 2 cups diced or shredded cooked chicken
- 1 cup shredded cheddar cheese
- green onions, to taste

Direction

- Preheat the oven to 350F
- In a medium bowl, stir together the cream cheese and hot sauce until well blended.
- Mix in the Ranch dressing and chicken.
- Spread into a 9x13 inch baking dish or deep pie plate.
- Sprinkle cheddar cheese on top.
- Bake for 30 minutes. Cool.
- Top with green onions.
- Serve with tortilla strips.

3. Baked Spinach Crab And Artichoke Dip Recipe

Serving: 24 | Cook: 20mins

Ingredients

- 1- cup mayonnaise   (or salad dressing like Miracle Whip)
- 1- cup freshly grated parmesan cheese
- 1- can (14 ounces) artichoke hearts drained and chopped coarsely
- 1 -package (10 ounces) frozen chopped spinach, thawed and squeezed to drain..
- 1 -package (8 ounces) fresh or imitation crabmeat chunks
- 1- 1/2 cups shredded pepper-jack cheese ....or (cheddar - cheese)
- toasted baguette slices and assorted gourmet crackers...

Direction

- Heat oven to 350 degrees f.

- Mix mayonnaise and parmesan cheese in a medium bowl
- Stir in artichoke hearts, spinach and crabmeat
- Spoon mixture into a 1 quart casserole dish ....sprinkle with pepper jack cheese
- Cover and bake 15- 20 minutes or until cheese is melted, and bubbly and heated thru
- Serve warm with baguette slices and crackers

4. Baked Spinach Artichoke Dip Recipe

Serving: 24 | Cook: 30mins

Ingredients

- 1 cup mayonnaise or salad dressing
- 1 cup freshly grated parmesan cheese
- 1 can (about 14 oz) artichoke hearts, drained and coarsely chopped
- 1 box (9oz) frozen spinach, thawed and squeezed to drain
- 1/2 cup chopped red bell pepper
- 1/4 cup shredded Monterey Jack or mozzarella cheese (1oz)
- toasted baguette slices or assorted crackers, if desired

Direction

- Heat oven to 350*F. Mix mayonnaise and parmesan cheese. Stir in artichokes, spinach, and bell pepper.
- Spoon mixture into 1 quart casserole. Sprinkle with Monterey Jack cheese.
- Cover and bake about 20 minutes or until cheese is melted. Serve warm with baguette slices.
- Makes 24 servings (2tablespoons each)

5. Bongo Dip Recipe

Serving: 8 | Cook: 15mins

Ingredients

- 1 cup mayonnaise
- 1 cup sour cream
- 10 ounce package chopped spinach thawed and drained
- 1 small can water chestnuts chopped fine
- 1 small onion chopped fine
- 1 envelope dry vegetable soup mix
- 1 cup mild shredded cheddar cheese

Direction

- Combine first six ingredients in a bowl and mix well.
- Put mixture into shallow baking dish then sprinkle cheese on top.
- Bake at 375 for 15 minutes or until cheese is completely melted.
- Serve immediately with hot garlic bread.

6. Braunschweiger Dips Recipe

Serving: 4

Ingredients

- 1 (8 ounce) roll braunschweiger
- 1 cup sour cream
- 1/2 envelope blue cheese salad dressing mix
- other add on if you would like! (maybe not!)
- 1 cup shredded mexican cheese (or your choice)
- 3 jalapeno pepper chopped (use gloves)

Direction

- Blend all ingredients together. Chill.
- Serve with radishes, green onions, also try potato chips, cucumbers, carrot sticks or crackers.

7. CROCK POT BEAN DIP Recipe

Serving: 1012 | Cook: 63mins

Ingredients

- VELVETTA cheese
- CAN OF rotel
- REFIRED beans
- hamburger
- tortilla chips

Direction

- BROWN GROUND BEEF
- CUBE VELVEETA CHEESE AND PLACE IN SLOW COOKER WITH BROWNED BEEF
- ADD ROTEL AND REFRIES
- MIX
- COOK ON MEDIUM TO LOW UNTIL HOT AND MELTED THRU.
- DIP TORTILLA CHIPS!
- YUMMY

8. Cajun Cheese Dip Recipe

Serving: 4 | Cook: 5mins

Ingredients

- 1 lb. of Andouille sausage (or other spicy sausage)
- 1/4 cup onion
- 1/8 cup cilantro and jalapenos to taste
- 2 lbs. Velveeta cheese

Direction

- Brown, drain, and crumble sausage. Mince onion, cilantro, and jalapenos.
- Combine all ingredients and cook in the microwave or on a double boiler until heated all the way through.
- Serve with toast points, crackers, chips, or tortillas.

9. California Bean Dip Recipe

Serving: 32

Ingredients

- 2 (11 oz) cans of white corn, liquid removed
- 2 (15 oz) cans of black beans, liquid removed and rinsed
- 1 cup ranch salad dressing
- 1/2 cup Italian salad dressing
- 1 small onion, chopped
- 1 tsp fresh cilantro, chopped
- 1 tsp chili powder
- 1 tsp hot pepper sauce
- 1/2 tsp ground black pepper

Direction

- Combine white corn, black beans, ranch and Italian dressing, onion, cilantro, chili powder, hot pepper sauce and ground black pepper, mix thoroughly. Place in the refrigerator, and chill for 8 hours (or overnight) before serving. Remove, and serve with chips.

10. Catalina Dip Recipe

Serving: 2

Ingredients

- 1 pkg cream cheese (let soften) (8 oz)
- 1 bttl Catalina salad dressing (small)
- 2 - 3 T catsup

Direction

- Mix all ingredients together.

Bravo! Top 50 Dip Recipes
Volume 10

Mary R. Smith

Copyright: Published in the United States by Mary R. Smith/ © MARY R. SMITH

Published on June, 18 2021

All rights reserved. No part of this publication may be reproduced, stored in retrieval system, copied in any form or by any means, electronic, mechanical, photocopying, recording or otherwise transmitted without written permission from the publisher. Please do not participate in or encourage piracy of this material in any way. You must not circulate this book in any format. MARY R. SMITH does not control or direct users' actions and is not responsible for the information or content shared, harm and/or actions of the book readers.

In accordance with the U.S. Copyright Act of 1976, the scanning, uploading and electronic sharing of any part of this book without the permission of the publisher constitute unlawful piracy and theft of the author's intellectual property. If you would like to use material from the book (other than just simply for reviewing the book), prior permission must be obtained by contacting the author at author@macadamiarecipes.com

Thank you for your support of the author's rights.

- Serve with raw veggies such as celery, carrots, green pepper, mushrooms, broccoli, cauliflower, etc.

11. Cheese Dip Recipe

Serving: 12 | Cook: 20mins

Ingredients

- 1 lb ground beef or chuck
- 1 lb ground sausage
- 1 can cream of mushroom soup
- 1 can rotel
- 2 lbs of Velvetta cheese, cubed

Direction

- Mix beef and sausage, fry and drain. In slow cooker add all ingredients; stir and cook until cheese is melted.

12. Cheesy Spinach Bacon Dip Recipe

Serving: 10 | Cook: 10mins

Ingredients

- 10 oz Pkg frozen chopped spinach, thawed and drained
- 16 oz Velveeta cheese, cut into cubes
- 4oz cream cheese
- 10 oz Can rotel -Diced tomatoes and green chilies, undrained
- 8 Slices Cooked bacon, crumbled

Direction

- In microwave safe bowl, combine all ingredients
- Microwave on high 6 mins, stirring every 2
- Heat until cheese is melted and well blended.

- Excellent to Serve in Bread Bowl - see post for Dip Bread Bowl.
- Also, good served with tortillas or bagels cut into piece
- Enjoy.

13. Chili Cheese Dip Recipe

Serving: 16 | Cook: 30mins

Ingredients

- 2 1/2 lbs. ground beef
- 2 cans (10oz) enchilada sauce (1 can for thicker dip)
- 2 cans (16oz) ranch style beans
- 2 can (10oz) tomatoes and green chilies (rotel)
- 2 envelopes chili mix, 1 regular, 1 hot
- 2 lbs Velveeta cheese, cubed
- 1 cup heavy whipping cream
- corn chips

Direction

- Cook beef over medium heat until done; drain.
- Add enchilada sauce, beans, tomatoes and chili mix; heat through.
- Add cheese and cream; cook until cheese is melted.
- Serve over chips.

14. Chilled Crab Dip Recipe

Serving: 8 | Cook: 70mins

Ingredients

- 2 (8oz) packages cream cheese, softened
- 1 pound cooked crab meat
- 1/2 cup creamy salad dressing (Miracle Whip)
- 1 (12oz) jar cocktail sauce

Direction

- In a medium bowl, mix together cream cheese, crab meat and creamy salad dressing. Chill in the refrigerator at least one hour. Cover with cocktail sauce before serving.

15. Corn Bread Dip Recipe

Serving: 8 | Cook: 35mins

Ingredients

- 2 boxes Jiffy cornbread mix (Cooked by directions on box)
- 1 onion, chopped
- 1 bell pepper, chopped
- ! can Rotel tomatoes
- 1 can mexicorn
- 2 cans chicken broth
- 12 oz grated cheddar cheese

Direction

- Mix and cook cornbread according to package directions.
- Sauté onion and bell pepper until tender.
- Crumble cornbread and add Rotel, mexicorn, chicken broth, and cheese to onion and pepper mixture.
- Place in a greased baking dish.
- Bake at 350 degrees until firm.

16. Cottage Cheese Dip Recipe

Serving: 12

Ingredients

- 1 ctn cottage cheese
- 1 (3 oz) package cream cheese, softened
- 1 tsp worcestershire sauce
- 1 T grated onion
- 2T salad dressing/Miracle Whip
- garlic salt to taste

Direction

- Mix all ingredients well and let stand overnight.
- Serve with crackers or chips.

17. Fiesta Corn Dip Recipe

Serving: 2 | Cook: 20mins

Ingredients

- 1 c. mayo or salad dressing
- 1 c. grated parmesan cheese
- 1 can of Fiesta corn, drained
- 1 8oz package of pepper Jack cheese, grated

Direction

- Mix all and Bake at 350 for 20 minutes or until heated through.
- Serve with Fritos Scoops

18. Football Dip Recipe

Serving: 12 | Cook: 20mins

Ingredients

- 1 large block of Mexician style Velveeta cheese
- 1 large bottle of picante salsa
- 1 package of conechu sausage
- 1 large bag of chips.

Direction

- Cube cheese and put into a medium size double boiler.
- Add picante salsa, let it cook slowly.
- Put sausage on the grill and cook until done.
- Slice sausage up and add to cheese mixture.
- When cheese is melted, the dip is ready.

19. Franks RedHot Buffalo Chicken Dip Recipe

Serving: 4 | Cook: 20mins

Ingredients

- 1 pkg. (8 ounces) cream cheese, softened
- 1/2 cup blue cheese salad dressing
- 1/2 cup any flavor Frank's® RedHot® Sauce
- 1/2 cup crumbled blue cheese or shredded mozzarella cheese (about 2 ounces)
- 2 cans (9.75 ounces each) Swanson® Premium Chunk chicken breast in water, drained
- assorted fresh vegetables or crackers or pita chips or pretzel rods

Direction

- Heat the oven to 350°F.
- Stir the cream cheese in a 9-inch deep dish pie plate with a fork or whisk until it's smooth.
- Stir in the dressing, sauce and blue cheese.
- Stir in the chicken.
- Bake for 20 minutes or until the chicken mixture is hot and bubbling.
- Stir before serving.
- Serve with the vegetables and crackers for dipping.
- To make in the microwave: Use a microwavable 9-inch deep dish pie plate. Prepare the dip as directed above in Step 2. Microwave, uncovered, on HIGH for 5 minutes or until the chicken mixture is hot, stirring halfway through the cook time.
- Tip: This dip can be kept warm in a small crockpot or fondue pot on the buffet table.

20. Hissy Fit Dip Recipe

Cook: 1hours

Ingredients

- Texas Recipes
- Hissy Fit Dip
- by Libby Murphy
- Ingredients:
- ...16 ounces sour cream
- 8 ounces cream cheese, softened
- 8 ounces Velveeta®, small cubed
- 1 cup white American cheese, shredded
- 1/2 - 1 pound pork sausage, crumbled, cooked and drained
- 1/4 cup green onion, finely chopped
- 1 teaspoon worcestershire sauce
- 1 teaspoon onion powder
- 1/2 teaspoon ground sage
- 1/4 teaspoon curry
- 1/8 teaspoon cayenne pepper
- Dash of garlic salt or powder
- sea salt and fresh cracked pepper to taste

Direction

- Directions:
- In a mixing bowl, combine all ingredients; stirring until well blended.
- Place in baking dish you have sprayed with non-stick coating.
- Bake at 350 degrees for 1 hour.
- Serve with crackers, chips, or veggie sticks – carrots, celery, sliced cauliflower, etc.
- Rumour has it that the first time this was served at an SEC tailgating party; it was so popular that it was gone in no time flat! One uppity Southern belle who missed tasting the new recipe was distraught and pitched a big hissy fit, hence forth the name.

21. Hot As Devil Pitchfork Pepper Dip Recipe

Serving: 4 | Cook: 45mins

Ingredients

- 3-4 green bell peppers seeded and chopped (don't use red or yellow peppers for this)
- 1/4 lbs - 1/2 lbs jalapenos sliced and keep the seeds
- 1 16oz can tomato puree
- a few red peppers flakes (optional)
- 1/4 cup of white or red wine vinegar
- pinch of sugar if tomato puree isn't sweet
- Optional
- fresh basil or parsley added towards the end of cooking

Direction

- Sauté the peppers in a pan over medium heat until softened (about 15 minutes). Season with salt if desired and then add the tomato puree, vinegar and a pinch of sugar if needed (I've never added any but I use good tomato puree) Simmer for 30 to 45 or until the sauce has thicken.
- Serve this as you would salsa with corn chips, pita chips or bread.

22. Hot Sausage Party Dip Recipe

Serving: 10 | Cook: 30mins

Ingredients

- 1 pound ground hot pork sausage
- 1 (10-ounce) can diced tomato and green chiles (rotel)
- 1 (8-ounce) package cream cheese, softened
- 3/4 cup (3 ounces) shredded sharp cheddar cheese
- corn chips

Direction

- Cook sausage in a large skillet, stirring until no longer pink; drain well.
- Drain diced tomato and green chilies, reserving 1/4 cup liquid.
- Stir together sausage, diced tomato and green chilies, reserved liquid, and cream cheese.
- Spoon into a lightly greased 1-quart baking dish; sprinkle with Cheddar cheese.
- Bake at 350° for 20 to 25 minutes or until bubbly.
- Serve with corn chips.

23. Hot Spinach Dip Recipe

Serving: 56

Ingredients

- 1 (10 oz) package frozen spinach, thawed and with liquid removed, chopped
- 2 cups monterey jack cheese, shredded
- 1 (16 oz) jar salsa
- 1 (2.25 oz) can black olives, drained and chopped
- 1 (8 oz) package cream cheese, softened and finely chopped
- 1 cup evaporated milk
- 1 tbsp red wine vinegar
- salt and pepper (to taste)

Direction

- Preheat oven to 400 degrees F.
- Combine spinach, jack cheese, salsa, cream cheese, olives, evaporated milk, black olives, red wine vinegar, salt and pepper in a medium baking dish.
- Bake for 12-15 minutes, or until bubbly.

24. Janets Black Bean Salsa Recipe

Serving: 12

Ingredients

- 1 15 oz can black beans, drained and rinsed
- 1 11 oz can white shoepeg corn

- 1/2 cup chopped green pepper
- 1/2 cup chopped onion
- 1 large tomato, diced
- 1/2 tsp. garlic powder
- Dressing:
- 1/2 cup zesty Italian salad dressing
- 3/4 tsp. tabasco
- 1/2 tsp. chili powder
- 1 Tablespoon cilantro

Direction

- Mix together the first six ingredients. Then mix together the dressing. Pour the dressing over the other ingredients and stir gently.

25. Jimmy Dean Dip Recipe

Serving: 20 | Cook: 20mins

Ingredients

- 2 packages Jimmy Dean sausage
- 2 cream cheese
- 1 large sour cream
- 1 onion
- 1 can diced olives
- 1 jar or fresh sliced jalapenos

Direction

- Dice the onion, and cook until translucent.
- Add the sausage and cook until done.
- Drain the sausage, and then put everything in the crock pot to simmer until it is all melted and simmering.
- Serve as an appetizer with Tostitos scoops.

26. Knorr Spinach Dip Recipe

Serving: 25 | Cook: 120mins

Ingredients

- 1 package (10 oz) baby spinach, chopped or 1 package (10 oz) frozen chopped spinach, thawed and squeezed dry
- 1 container (16 oz) sour cream
- 1 cup mayonnaise (I use Miracle Whip and I think it's better!)
- 1 package Knorr vegetable recipe soup mix
- 1 can (8 oz) water chestnuts, drained and chopped (optional, but recommended...gives that extra added crunch)
- 3 green onions, chopped (optional)

Direction

- Combine all ingredients and chill about 2 hours.
- Serve with your favorite dippers. Vegetables and club crackers are the best!

27. Mexican Sausage Dip Recipe

Serving: 6 | Cook: 5mins

Ingredients

- 1 pkg. Jimmy Dean's hot sausage
- 8 oz. Velveeta cheese, cut into chunks
- 1 can Ro-tell (original)mtomatoes
- Mix together, warm and serve in chafing dish.
- serve with crackers, nacho chips, whatever you desire.

Direction

- We will number these for you! Just hit 'enter' after every step.

28. Ms. Pringles Bean Dip Recipe

Serving: 12 | Cook: 10mins

Ingredients

- 2-30oz. cans Refried beans(or 4-16oz cans)
- 10-12 oz of Velveeta
- 1 lb Jimmy Dean breakfast Sausage(fully cooked)

Direction

- Combine above ingredients in a slow cooker and heat on low until the cheese has melted sufficiently to combine.
- Serve with chips or works well in burritos.

29. New Mexico Spinach Dip Recipe

Serving: 8 | Cook: 35mins

Ingredients

- olive oil
- 1 onion, chopped
- 1 14.5 oz. can diced tomatoes
- 1 4 oz. can green chilies, drained
- 1 10 oz. pkg. frozen spinach, thawed and drained
- 1 8 oz. pkg. cream cheese, softened
- 1 cup half half
- 1 1/2 cups Mexican blend or monterey jack cheese
- 1 tbls. red wine vinegar
- 2 tbls. sour cream
- salt and pepper to taste

Direction

- Preheat oven to 400
- In pan, heat olive oil and sauté onion until tender
- Add tomatoes and chilies and then cook a minute or so
- In large mixing bowl, add all ingredients and stir until blended completely
- Put mixture in an 8x8 baking dish
- Bake 35 minutes or so

30. Queso Dip Recipe

Serving: 12 | Cook: 2hours

Ingredients

- 1 32oz block Velveeta
- 1 8oz cream cheese
- 1 10oz Rotel
- 1 can soup- cream of mushroom, chicken, or onion
- 1 lb ground beef or sausage
- 1 green onion, optional

Direction

- Brown ground beef or sausage. Cut up Velveeta and cream cheese into cubes and place in crock pot. Pour Rotel and soup over cheese. Place on low setting for an hour, allow ingredients to meld. Add browned meat and onion and continue on low for at least 30 more minutes.
- Serve with crackers, chips, veggies, be creative!

31. Ranch Bean Dip Recipe

Serving: 8 | Cook: 10mins

Ingredients

- 1 (16 oz) can refried beans
- 1 (1 oz) packet of dry ranch dressing mix
- 1 cup sour cream
- 2 cups cheddar cheese, shredded

Direction

- Combine the beans, dressing mix, sour cream and cheese in a small saucepan. Heat the mixture over medium heat, stirring until they are warm and blended well. Serve.

32. Ro Tel Dip Recipe

Serving: 10 | Cook: 15mins

Ingredients

- 1 lb. ground beef
- 1 medium onion, chopped
- 1 bell pepper, chopped (optional)
- 1 - 2 lb. box Velveeta cheese, cubed
- 2 cans rotel diced tomatoes and chilies (mild or hot)
- 1 large can chili hot beans, undrained
- 1 small jar jalapeno pepper rings, drained (optional)
- 2 large bags tortilla chips

Direction

- Brown ground beef, onion and bell pepper. Drain.
- Pour Rotel tomatoes into a Dutch oven and put cubed Velveeta cheese into tomatoes. Heat on medium-low heat until cheese is completely melted. Stirring frequently.
- Stir in ground beef mixture and chili hot beans.
- Heat thoroughly.
- Add jalapeno peppers and serve with tortilla chips.

33. Rootie Tootie Party Bean Dip Recipe

Serving: 10 | Cook: 37mins

Ingredients

- 2 large can chili with beans
- 4 pre-cooked breakfast sausage patties, crumbled
- 1 large block of Velveeta cheese
- 1 T. canned jalapeno pieces
- tortilla chips

Direction

- In crock pot, mix all ingredients (except chips) and let simmer on medium for 35-40 minutes until all melty and bubbly.
- Serve with tortilla chips.

34. Ruben Dip Recipe

Serving: 15 | Cook: 60mins

Ingredients

- 1 pound corned beef, chopped (lunch sandwich style)
- 1 small sourkraut (drained)
- 8 oz cream cheese, softened
- 1 cup mayonnaise
- 1 pound swiss cheese shredded
- 1/2 cup 1000 island dressing
- 1 can water chestnuts, drained and chopped fine

Direction

- Combine all of the above ingredients.
- Stuff into a large pumpernickel loaf that's been hollowed out.
- Wrap well in foil and bake for 1 hour at 350 degrees.
- Cut the hollowed centre pieces to bite size and serve on a large platter with the chunks surrounding the stuffed pumpernickel loaf.
- You will probably need extra bread to go with this...

35. Sausage Beef Rotel Dip Recipe

Serving: 12 | Cook: 20mins

Ingredients

- 1 lb. ground beef
- 1 lb. sausage, casings removed
- 1 medium onion, chopped
- 1 lb. pasteurized process cheese spread, cubed
- 1 can (10 oz.) RO*TEL diced tomatoes green chilies, undrained
- 1 teaspoon garlic powder

Direction

- In a large skillet, brown beef, sausage and onion; drain.
- Add remaining ingredients; stir over low heat until cheese spread is melted.
- Serve warm with tortilla chips.
- Keep warm in a medium crock pot - for best results

36. Sausage Dip Recipe

Serving: 10 | Cook: 10mins

Ingredients

- 2 8 oz. packages of Philadelphia cream cheese
- 1 can rotel
- 1 lb Jimmy Dean Mild sausage

Direction

- Crumble sausage and brown in skillet, drain.
- Place both packages of cream cheese in microwave safe bowl. Pour Rotel on top. Microwave on high until cheese is soft enough to stir and mix with Rotel. Place back in microwave for approximately 2 minutes, stir.
- Slowly stir sausage into mixture.
- Serve with Tortilla chips!
- (For spicier dip you can use Jimmy Dean Hot Sausage instead!)

37. Spicey Sausage Cream Cheese Dip Recipe

Serving: 10 | Cook: 12mins

Ingredients

- 2 packages cream cheese (room temp)
- 1 lb package Hot pork sausage
- 1 can Original Rotel tomatoes w/ green Chiles
- 3 green onions Chopped
- 2 cloves garlic minced
- Frito's Scoops

Direction

- Place Cream Cheese in a small crock pot and turn on low.
- Cook Sausage until browned in a heavy skillet, over med high. When sufficiently browned, drain Sausage and add Green Onion and Garlic and cook 2 minutes more.
- Add the Rotel Tomatoes w/ Green Chiles. Stir until mixture is hot and bubbling.
- Add Hot Sausage mixture to the crock pot with Cream Cheese.
- Mix well.
- Keep on low setting and serve with Frito's Scoops

38. Spicy Cheese Dip Recipe

Serving: 8 | Cook: 15mins

Ingredients

- 1/2 big block of reg Velveeta cheese
- 1 can Ro-Tel

Direction

- Cut 1/2 block of cheese into smaller chunks, place in sauce pan, pour in can of Ro-Tel, juice and all. Cook on LOW till all melted. Serve with tortilla chips!

- Also can be done in microwave, on a low setting.
- This dip is very easy to burn.

39. Spicy Sausage Garlic Dip Recipe

Serving: 8 | Cook: 10mins

Ingredients

- 1 lb pork sausage
- 1 (10 oz) frozen chopped spinach-thawed
- 1 (8oz) cream cheese-softened
- 1 cup sour cream
- 1 cup shredded cheddar cheese
- 1/2 cup chopped green onions
- 1 (10 oz) diced tomatoes with green chilies
- 1 sm can green chilies (to your heat preference)
- 1 tsp garlic powder
- 2 cloves garlic minced

Direction

- Cook sausage
- Drain
- Add 2Tbs. water cover and cook 1 minute
- Thaw spinach and squeeze until dry
- Crumble spinach into pork sausage and add rest of ingredients
- Stir and cook until heated through and cheeses are melted
- Serve in warm bread bowl with bread bits torn up tortilla chips for dipping.

40. Super Bowl Dip Recipe

Serving: 1 | Cook: 10mins

Ingredients

- *Pre-heat crockpot
- 2 lbs. roll sausage
- 2 cans Ro-tel or one large jar salsa, use hot!!BETTER
- 1 large Velvetta cheese, cut into cubes

Direction

- In skillet, brown sausage drain grease. Dump cheese into crockpot with the cans of Rotel and add sausage. Stir until blended, after cheese has melted, stir again and set crockpot on low.
- Serve with tortilla chips or bagel rounds. Stays hot in crockpot.
- VARIATION: use 2 lbs. ground beef and Taco Seasoning Mix (your own or store bought.) Brown ground beef and add taco seasoning. Add into crockpot with Rotel and Velveeta.

41. Super Bowl Salsa Dip Recipe

Serving: 80 | Cook: 90mins

Ingredients

- 2 pounds Velveeta, cubed
- 1/2 cup milk
- 1 pound spicy italian sausage
- 1 onion, chopped
- 1 can rotel
- 1 (12 oz) jar medium salsa (I like to use spicy)
- 1/2 can black beans, drained and rinsed
- 1 bunch green onions
- tortilla chips

Direction

- In a slow cooker set to high, place the cheese and milk and cook stirring occasionally until the cheese has melted and is well blended with the milk
- Cook Sausage until evenly brown, add onions and cook until onion is translucent
- Remove from heat and drain off grease
- Stir sausage mixture into cheese mixture
- Reduce heat to low
- Mix in salsa, Rotel and black beans

- Cook for about an hour, stirring occasionally
- Garnish with green onions and serve with tortilla chips

42. Super Sausage Dip Recipe

Serving: 6 | Cook: 35mins

Ingredients

- 1lb. bulk pork sausage
- 1 small onion, chopped
- 1/2c. chopped green pepper
- 3 medium tomatoes, chopped
- 1-4oz. can chopped green chilies
- 1-8oz. pk. cream cheese, cubed
- 16oz. sour cream
- tortilla chips

Direction

- In a large skillet, cook the sausage, onion and green pepper over medium heat until the meat is no longer pink; drain.
- Add the tomatoes and green chilies; mix well. Bring to a boil. Reduce heat; simmer, uncovered, for 30 minutes, stirring occasionally.
- Add the cream cheese; stir until melted. Stir in sour cream.
- Transfer to a fondue pot and keep warm.
- Serve with tortilla chips.

43. Sweet Tomato Chutney Recipe

Cook: 180mins

Ingredients

- 1 whole head garlic, peeled chopped
- One 2-inch piece of fresh ginger (1 inch by 1 inch), peeled and chopped
- 1-1/2 cups red wine vinegar
- 2 pounds fresh skinned tomatoes (or 1 pound and 12 ounces canned whole tomatoes)
- 1-1/2 cups granulated sugar
- 1-1/2 teaspoon salt
- 1/4 to 1/2 teaspoon cayenne pepper (depending on how hot you like it)
- 2 Tablespoons golden raisins
- 2 Tablespoons blanched slivered almonds

Direction

- Put the garlic, ginger and 1/2 cup of vinegar in the food processor and process until smooth.
- In a large, heavy-bottomed pot, place the tomatoes (and juice from the can if using canned tomatoes) and the rest of the vinegar, sugar, salt, cayenne. Bring to a boil.
- Add the puree from the food processor and simmer uncovered for about 2 to 3 hours until it thickens and a film clings to a spoon when dipped.
- Stir occasionally at first and more frequently later as it thickens. You may need to lower the heat as the liquid diminishes.
- Add almonds and raisins. Simmer, stirring another 5 minutes. Turn off the heat and let cool.
- It should be as thick as honey. Bottle in clean containers, and refrigerate. Must be kept in the refrigerator. Good indefinitely. Makes about 2 cups.
- This is great served with cream cheese and crackers

44. Ultimate Spinach Dip Recipe

Serving: 8 | Cook: 120mins

Ingredients

- 1 package (10 oz) chopped spinach, thawed and squeezed dry.
- 1 container (16 oz.) sour cream

- 1 cup Hellmans's or Best Foods Real Mayonaise
- 1 package Knorr vegetable Recipe mix
- 1 can (8 oz) water chestnuts, drained and chopped(optional)
- 3 green onions, chopped(optional)
- 1 tub(12 oz) Philadelphia whipped cream cheese
- 1 bunch of cilantro chopped and stems removed
- 1 STEEL BOWL to Mix and Store in

Direction

- If you don't have a steel bowl with a lid, this is one good reason to go and buy one! You just can't get the dip as cold in anything else and COLD keeps everything crispy longer.
- Simply mix all of the ingredients above in a steel bowl to combine well. Cover and chill for at least 2 hours before serving with your favorite chips. Also good in Tortilla rollups, burgers, shucks it goes good on everything!

45. Vegetable Dip Recipe

Cook: 15mins

Ingredients

- 1 cup sour cream
- 4 oz. cream cheese
- 2 tablespoons Hellmann's mayonnaise
- 1 pkg hidden valley ranch dressing mix
- Pinch of red pepper or a dash of Tabasco sauce.

Direction

- Mix well
- Chill

46. Velveeta Rotel Dip Recipe

Serving: 6 | Cook: 15mins

Ingredients

- 1 lb. ground beef
- 2 (10 oz) cans Ro-Tel mild diced tomatoes green chilies (drained)
- 2 lbs. Kraft Velveeta

Direction

- Cook ground beef and drain well.
- Cut Velveeta into 1 inch chunks and put into sauce pan, over low heat.
- Stir in Ro-Tel, and cooked beef.
- Cook over low, stirring often, until cheese is melted. If mixture is too thick, add 1-2 tablespoons of milk.
- Serve with corn chips and enjoy.

47. Weasel Dip Recipe

Serving: 8 | Cook: 10mins

Ingredients

- 1 8oz. pkg. cream cheese
- 1 can Rotel tomatoes
- 1/2lb. lean ground beef
- 1/2lb. lean pork sausage

Direction

- Brown meat in skillet. Drain well. Return to skillet; add cream cheese, and Rotel tomatoes. Heat until bubbly. Great dip nacho chips

48. Zesty Salsa Recipe

Serving: 15 | Cook: 60mins

Ingredients

- 2 large tomatoes, diced
- 6 green onions, chopped
- 1 cup finely shredded monterey jack cheese
- 1 (4 ounce) can chopped green chilies
- 1 (2.25 ounce) can sliced ripe olives, drained
- 1 T chopped garlic
- 1/4 cup Italian salad dressing

Direction

- In a bowl, combine the first seven ingredients; mix well. Cover and refrigerate for at least 1 hour.

49. Buffalo Chicken Dip Recipe

Serving: 8 | Cook: 17mins

Ingredients

- 4 boneless skinless chicken breasts
- 1 1 2. oz. bottle Frank's buffalo wind sauce
- 2 8 oz. blocks cream cheese
- 1 16 oz. bottle ranch dressing
- 1 bag of shredded cheese

Direction

- Poach chicken breasts until done and shreds easy
- Shred chicken breasts and place into baking dish
- Pour buffalo wing sauce onto chicken and mix
- Melt cream cheese and ranch dressing in pan
- Pour mixture on top on chicken
- Top with shredded cheese
- Place dish into oven 325 and cook until cheese melts and is bubbling
- Enjoy!

50. Creamy Italian Dip Recipe

Serving: 6

Ingredients

- 1 cup Miracle Whip
- 1 cup sour cream
- 1 envelope Italian salad dressing
- 1/4 CUP CHOPPED RED AND green bell peppers

Direction

- Mix all ingredients until well blended, stir in peppers, cover.
- Refrigerate several hours till chilled.
- Serve with crackers or fresh veggies.

Index

A
almond 3,4,16

artichoke 3,4,5

B
bacon 3,7

bagel 7,15

baguette 4,5

baking 4,5,8,9,10,12,18

basil 10

beans 6,7,12,13

beef 3,6,7,12,13,14,15,17

black beans 6,10,15

black pepper 6

bread 3,5,7,8,10,13,15

broccoli 7

broth 8

burger 6,17

C
carrot 5,7,9

cauliflower 7,9

cayenne pepper 9,16

celery 7,9

cheddar 4,5,8,10,12,15

cheese 3,4,5,6,7,8,9,10,11,12,13,14,15,16,17,18

chicken 3,4,8,9,12,18

chips 5,6,7,8,9,10,11,12,13,14,15,16,17

chutney 3,16

cloves 14,15

cocktail 7,8

corned beef 13

cottage cheese 3,8

crab 3,4,5,7,8

crackers 4,5,6,8,9,11,12,16,18

cream 3,4,5,6,7,8,9,10,11,12,13,14,15,16,17,18

crumble 6,7,8,9,13,14,15

cucumber 5

curry 9

E
eel 17

egg 7,9,12,18

evaporated milk 10

G
garlic 3,5,8,9,11,14,15,16,18

gin 11,14,16

H
ham 6

hare 2

heart 4,5

honey 16

J
jus 2,11,17

L
ling 9,14,16,18

M
macadamia 2

mayonnaise 4,5,11,13,17

meat 4,5,7,8,12,16,17

milk 15,17

mince 6,14,15

mozzarella 5,9

mushroom 7,12

N

nut 4,5,8,9,10,12,13,14,15,16

O

oil 6,8,12,13,16

olive 10,11,12,18

onion 4,5,6,8,9,11,12,13,14,15,16,17,18

P

parmesan 4,5,8

parsley 10

peel 16

pepper 3,4,5,6,7,8,9,10,11,12,13,16,17,18

pie 2,4,7,9,13,16

pork 9,10,14,15,16,17

port 2

potato 5

R

radish 5

raisins 16

red wine 10,12,16

rum 9

S

sage 9

salad 4,5,6,7,8,9,11,18

salsa 3,8,10,15,17

salt 8,9,10,12,16

sausage 3,6,7,8,9,10,11,12,13,14,15,16,17

sea salt 9

seasoning 15

seeds 10

soup 5,7,11,12

spinach 3,4,5,7,10,11,12,15,16

sugar 10,16

T

tabasco 11,17

taco 15

tea 9,14,16

tomato 3,7,8,10,11,12,13,14,15,16,17,18

V

vegetables 9,11

vinegar 10,12,16

W

water chestnut 5,11,13,17

whipping cream 7

worcestershire sauce 8,9

Z

zest 3,11,17

Conclusion

Thank you again for downloading this book!

I hope you enjoyed reading about my book!

If you enjoyed this book, please take the time to share your thoughts and post a review on Amazon. It'd be greatly appreciated!

Write me an honest review about the book – I truly value your opinion and thoughts and I will incorporate them into my next book, which is already underway.

Thank you!

If you have any questions, **feel free to contact at:** *author@macadamiarecipes.com*

Mary R. Smith

macadamiarecipes.com

conversion chart
FOR THE KITCHEN

VOLUME MEASUREMENT CONVERSIONS

Cups	Tablespoons	Teaspoons	Milliliters
		1 tsp	5 ml
1/16 cup	1 tbsp	3 tsp	15 ml
1/8 cup	2 tbsp	6 tsp	30 ml
1/4 cup	4 tbsp	12 tsp	60 ml
1/3 cup	5 1/3 tbsp	16 tsp	80 ml
1/2 cup	8 tbsp	24 tsp	120 ml
2/3 cup	10 2/3 tbsp	32 tsp	160 ml
3/4 cup	12 tbsp	36 tsp	180 ml
1 cup	16 tbsp	48 tsp	240 ml

1 QUART =
2 pins
4 cups
32 ounces
950 ml

1 PINT =
2 cups
14 ounces
480 ml

1 CUP =
16 tbsp
8 ounces
240 ml

1/4 CUP =
4 tbsp
12 tsp
2 ounces
60 ml

1 TBSP =
3 tsp
1/2 ounce
15 ml

COOKING TEMPERATURE CONVERSIONS

Celcius/Centigrade   F = (Cx1.8) + 32
Fahrenheit   C = (F-32) x 0.5556

RECIPE:

COOKING TIME

RATING

SERVINGS

INGREDIENTS

INSTRUCTIONS

NOTES

RECIPE:

COOKING TIME | RATING | SERVINGS

INGREDIENTS

INSTRUCTIONS | NOTES

RECIPE:

COOKING TIME

RATING

SERVINGS

INGREDIENTS

INSTRUCTIONS

NOTES

RECIPE:

COOKING TIME | RATING | SERVINGS

INGREDIENTS

INSTRUCTIONS | NOTES

RECIPE:

COOKING TIME

RATING

SERVINGS

INGREDIENTS

INSTRUCTIONS

NOTES

RECIPE:

COOKING TIME

RATING

SERVINGS

INGREDIENTS

INSTRUCTIONS

NOTES

RECIPE:

COOKING TIME   **RATING**   **SERVINGS**

INGREDIENTS

INSTRUCTIONS   **NOTES**

RECIPE:

| COOKING TIME | RATING | SERVINGS |

INGREDIENTS

INSTRUCTIONS | NOTES

RECIPE:

COOKING TIME

RATING

SERVINGS

INGREDIENTS

INSTRUCTIONS

NOTES

RECIPE:

COOKING TIME

RATING

SERVINGS

INGREDIENTS

INSTRUCTIONS

NOTES

RECIPE:

COOKING TIME

RATING

SERVINGS

INGREDIENTS

INSTRUCTIONS

NOTES

RECIPE:

COOKING TIME

RATING

SERVINGS

INGREDIENTS

INSTRUCTIONS

NOTES

RECIPE:

COOKING TIME

RATING

SERVINGS

INGREDIENTS

INSTRUCTIONS

NOTES

RECIPE:

COOKING TIME

RATING

SERVINGS

INGREDIENTS

INSTRUCTIONS

NOTES

RECIPE:

COOKING TIME

RATING

SERVINGS

INGREDIENTS

INSTRUCTIONS

NOTES

RECIPE:

COOKING TIME **RATING** **SERVINGS**

INGREDIENTS

INSTRUCTIONS **NOTES**

RECIPE:

COOKING TIME

RATING

SERVINGS

INGREDIENTS

INSTRUCTIONS

NOTES

RECIPE:

COOKING TIME

RATING

SERVINGS

INGREDIENTS

INSTRUCTIONS

NOTES

RECIPE:

COOKING TIME **RATING** **SERVINGS**

INGREDIENTS

INSTRUCTIONS **NOTES**

RECIPE:

COOKING TIME

RATING

SERVINGS

INGREDIENTS

INSTRUCTIONS

NOTES

RECIPE:

COOKING TIME

RATING

SERVINGS

INGREDIENTS

INSTRUCTIONS

NOTES

RECIPE:

COOKING TIME | RATING | SERVINGS

INGREDIENTS

INSTRUCTIONS | NOTES

RECIPE:

COOKING TIME **RATING** **SERVINGS**

INGREDIENTS

INSTRUCTIONS **NOTES**

RECIPE:

COOKING TIME

RATING

SERVINGS

INGREDIENTS

INSTRUCTIONS

NOTES

RECIPE:

COOKING TIME

RATING

SERVINGS

INGREDIENTS

INSTRUCTIONS

NOTES

RECIPE:

COOKING TIME | **RATING** | **SERVINGS**

INGREDIENTS

INSTRUCTIONS | NOTES

RECIPE:

COOKING TIME

RATING

SERVINGS

INGREDIENTS

INSTRUCTIONS

NOTES

RECIPE:

COOKING TIME

RATING

SERVINGS

INGREDIENTS

INSTRUCTIONS

NOTES

RECIPE:

COOKING TIME

RATING

SERVINGS

INGREDIENTS

INSTRUCTIONS

NOTES

RECIPE:

COOKING TIME

RATING

SERVINGS

INGREDIENTS

INSTRUCTIONS

NOTES

RECIPE:

COOKING TIME

RATING

SERVINGS

INGREDIENTS

INSTRUCTIONS

NOTES

RECIPE:

COOKING TIME | RATING | SERVINGS

INGREDIENTS

INSTRUCTIONS | NOTES

RECIPE:

COOKING TIME | RATING | SERVINGS

INGREDIENTS

INSTRUCTIONS | NOTES

RECIPE:

COOKING TIME

RATING

SERVINGS

INGREDIENTS

INSTRUCTIONS

NOTES

RECIPE:

COOKING TIME

RATING

SERVINGS

INGREDIENTS

INSTRUCTIONS

NOTES

RECIPE:

COOKING TIME

RATING

SERVINGS

INGREDIENTS

INSTRUCTIONS

NOTES

RECIPE:

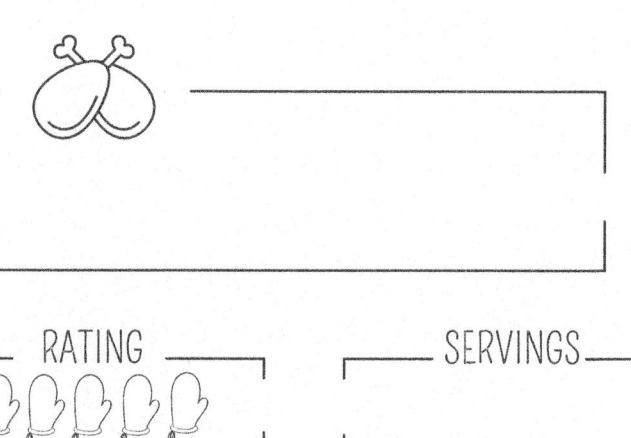

COOKING TIME | RATING | SERVINGS

INGREDIENTS

INSTRUCTIONS | NOTES

RECIPE:

COOKING TIME | **RATING** | **SERVINGS**

INGREDIENTS

INSTRUCTIONS | NOTES

RECIPE:

COOKING TIME

RATING

SERVINGS

INGREDIENTS

INSTRUCTIONS

NOTES

RECIPE:

COOKING TIME

RATING

SERVINGS

INGREDIENTS

INSTRUCTIONS

NOTES

RECIPE:

COOKING TIME **RATING** **SERVINGS**

INGREDIENTS

INSTRUCTIONS **NOTES**

RECIPE:

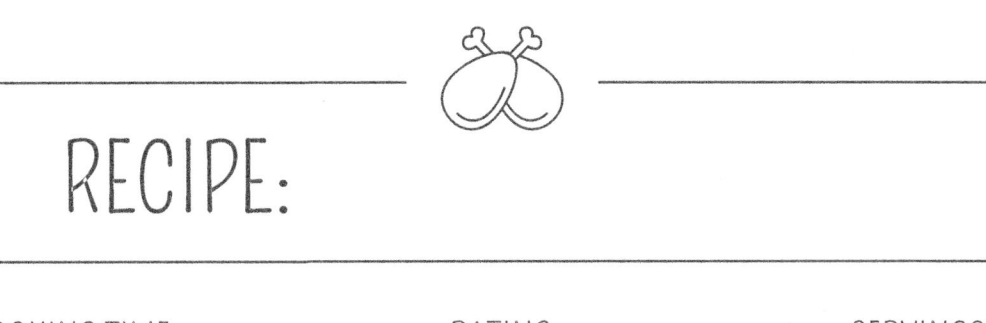

COOKING TIME **RATING** **SERVINGS**

INGREDIENTS

INSTRUCTIONS **NOTES**

RECIPE:

COOKING TIME **RATING** **SERVINGS**

INGREDIENTS

INSTRUCTIONS **NOTES**

RECIPE:

COOKING TIME

RATING

SERVINGS

INGREDIENTS

INSTRUCTIONS

NOTES

RECIPE:

COOKING TIME   **RATING**   **SERVINGS**

INGREDIENTS

INSTRUCTIONS   **NOTES**

RECIPE:

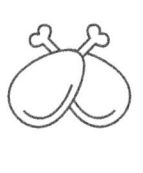

COOKING TIME

RATING

SERVINGS

INGREDIENTS

INSTRUCTIONS

NOTES

RECIPE:

COOKING TIME

RATING

SERVINGS

INGREDIENTS

INSTRUCTIONS

NOTES

RECIPE:

COOKING TIME **RATING** **SERVINGS**

INGREDIENTS

INSTRUCTIONS **NOTES**

RECIPE:

COOKING TIME | RATING | SERVINGS

INGREDIENTS

INSTRUCTIONS | NOTES

RECIPE:

COOKING TIME

RATING

SERVINGS

INGREDIENTS

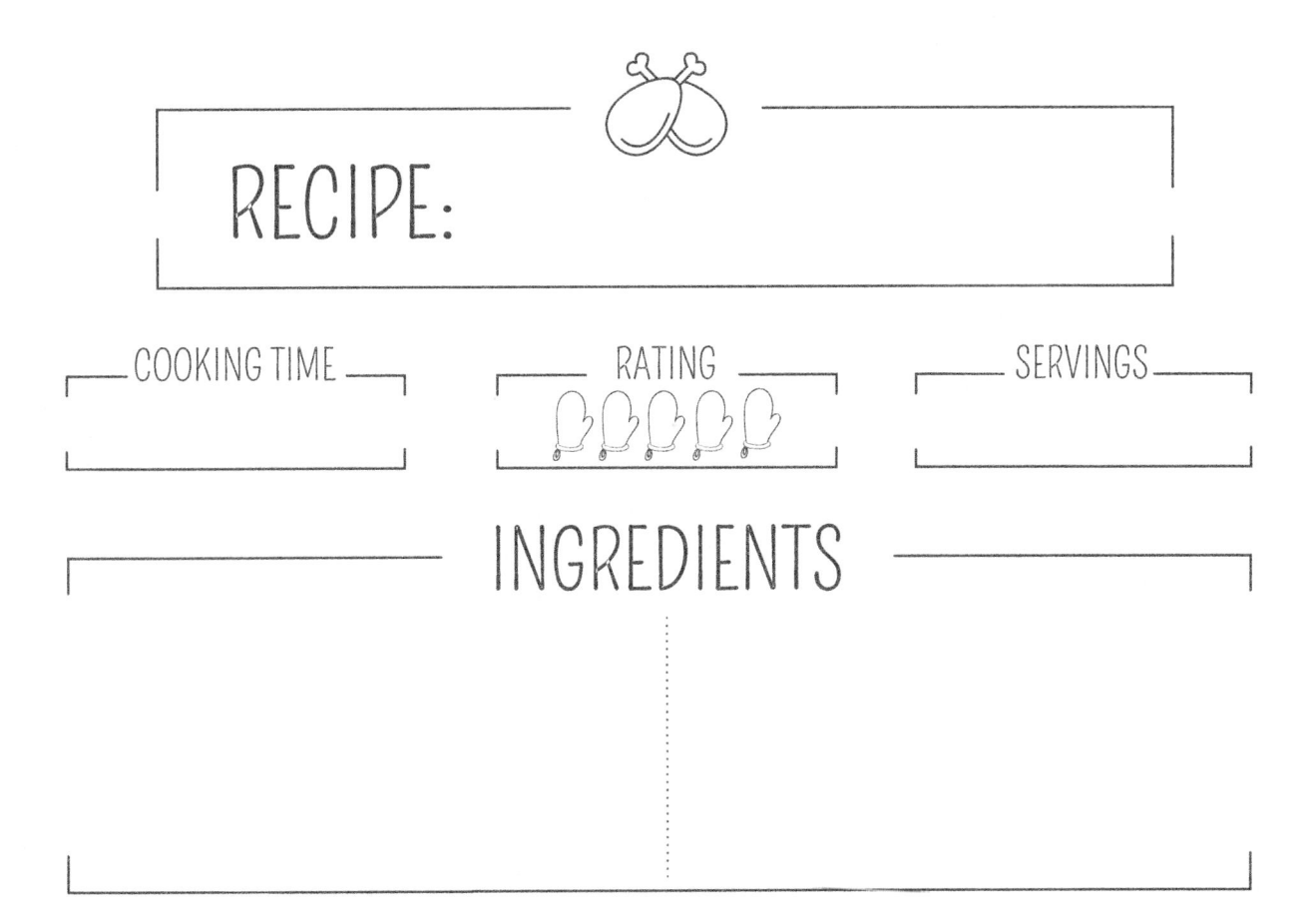

INSTRUCTIONS

NOTES

RECIPE:

COOKING TIME

RATING

SERVINGS

INGREDIENTS

INSTRUCTIONS

NOTES

RECIPE:

COOKING TIME

RATING

SERVINGS

INGREDIENTS

INSTRUCTIONS

NOTES

RECIPE:

COOKING TIME

RATING

SERVINGS

INGREDIENTS

INSTRUCTIONS

NOTES

RECIPE:

COOKING TIME

RATING

SERVINGS

INGREDIENTS

INSTRUCTIONS

NOTES

RECIPE:

COOKING TIME | RATING | SERVINGS

INGREDIENTS

INSTRUCTIONS | NOTES

RECIPE:

COOKING TIME

RATING

SERVINGS

INGREDIENTS

INSTRUCTIONS

NOTES

RECIPE:

COOKING TIME | RATING | SERVINGS

INGREDIENTS

INSTRUCTIONS | NOTES

RECIPE:

COOKING TIME **RATING** **SERVINGS**

INGREDIENTS

INSTRUCTIONS **NOTES**

RECIPE:

COOKING TIME | RATING | SERVINGS

INGREDIENTS

INSTRUCTIONS | NOTES

RECIPE:

COOKING TIME

RATING

SERVINGS

INGREDIENTS

INSTRUCTIONS

NOTES

RECIPE:

COOKING TIME

RATING

SERVINGS

INGREDIENTS

INSTRUCTIONS

NOTES

RECIPE:

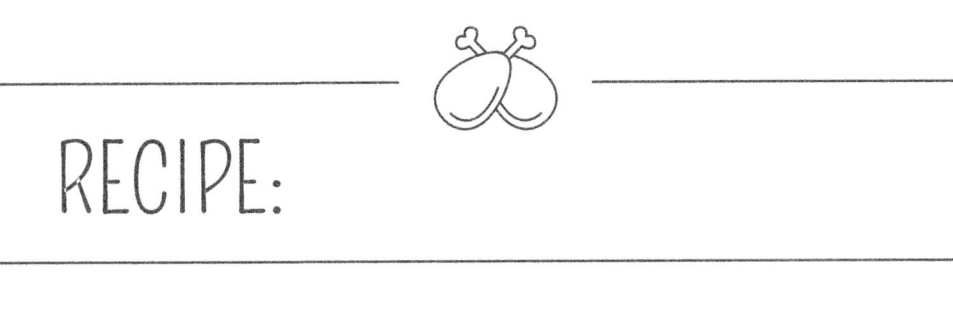

COOKING TIME

RATING

SERVINGS

INGREDIENTS

INSTRUCTIONS

NOTES

RECIPE:

COOKING TIME

RATING

SERVINGS

INGREDIENTS

INSTRUCTIONS

NOTES

RECIPE:

COOKING TIME

RATING

SERVINGS

INGREDIENTS

INSTRUCTIONS

NOTES

RECIPE:

COOKING TIME

RATING

SERVINGS

INGREDIENTS

INSTRUCTIONS

NOTES

RECIPE:

COOKING TIME

RATING

SERVINGS

INGREDIENTS

INSTRUCTIONS

NOTES

RECIPE:

COOKING TIME

RATING

SERVINGS

INGREDIENTS

INSTRUCTIONS

NOTES

RECIPE:

COOKING TIME

RATING

SERVINGS

INGREDIENTS

INSTRUCTIONS

NOTES

RECIPE:

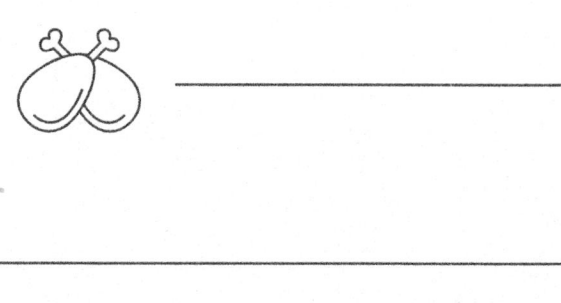

COOKING TIME

RATING

SERVINGS

INGREDIENTS

INSTRUCTIONS

NOTES

RECIPE:

COOKING TIME

RATING

SERVINGS

INGREDIENTS

INSTRUCTIONS

NOTES

RECIPE:

COOKING TIME

RATING

SERVINGS

INGREDIENTS

INSTRUCTIONS

NOTES

RECIPE:

COOKING TIME

RATING

SERVINGS

INGREDIENTS

INSTRUCTIONS

NOTES

RECIPE:

COOKING TIME

RATING

SERVINGS

INGREDIENTS

INSTRUCTIONS

NOTES

RECIPE:

COOKING TIME

RATING

SERVINGS

INGREDIENTS

INSTRUCTIONS

NOTES

RECIPE:

COOKING TIME

RATING

SERVINGS

INGREDIENTS

INSTRUCTIONS

NOTES

RECIPE:

COOKING TIME

RATING

SERVINGS

INGREDIENTS

INSTRUCTIONS

NOTES

RECIPE:

COOKING TIME

RATING

SERVINGS

INGREDIENTS

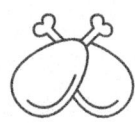

INSTRUCTIONS

NOTES

Printed in Great Britain
by Amazon